PeopleSoft Query
For
Grants Management

By

Herman J Pinto ACA, PMP

Copyright

Disclaimer

DEDICATION

I'd like to dedicate this book to all the people who have directly or indirectly influenced me over my career.

My Family & Friends

To my lovely wife Melanie, for all her support and my son Keegan for giving me the impetus to write.

To my loving father and mother for raising me to believe in myself.

To my siblings for their love and support.

To my friends all over the world – for their support

My Clients

To my clients – for challenging me with unique problems and supporting me as we resolved them.

PREFACE

I've been associated with financial systems for around 25 years as an Auditor, Finance Controller, Project Manager and Systems Integrator. Over the years all ERP Systems have moved in the direction of providing the functional user more control over data flow – entry and analysis.

PeopleSoft Financials 9.2 (Peopletools 8.83/8.54) is the latest success story by Oracle - giving the PeopleSoft functional user more flexibility and control in the design of reports, workflow and interfaces.

Query is one of the most powerful and flexible reporting tools in PeopleSoft and has become the feeder tool for several reporting and workflow channels within PeopleSoft. Mastering this tool should be the goal of every PeopleSoft user – functional and technical

Goals: My goals in writing this book are:
  a) Interest: To create an interest in Complex PeopleSoft Queries. Today many query users create basic queries – without covering complex applications. Some users download query results to Microsoft Excel to analyze their data.

b) Structured Approach: To provide all PeopleSoft users with basic structured training on PeopleSoft Query by creating actual queries in each chapter with increasing complexity.

c) Relationships: To provide an understanding of the importance of PeopleSoft Query to other tools and functions in PeopleSoft.

Approach: I have structured this book to provide step-by-step training under a case study, while explaining each step in context of PeopleSoft Financials. This book covers:

a) Understanding the basics of SQL (Structured Query Language) – the basis of PeopleSoft Query.
b) Creating a basic Query with "Joins" (XX_TRAIN_001)
c) Creating a query with "Prompts" (XX_TRAIN_002)
d) Creating a query with "Distinct" (XX_TRAIN_003)
e) Creating a query with "Expressions" (XX_TRAIN_004)
f) Reviewing the SQL behind the Queries that we created.
g) Creating a query with a simple example of a new feature in PeopleSoft 9.2 - "Transformations" through XSLT formatting (XX_TRAIN_005)

This book also provides a general understanding of Reporting tools with a focus on the role of PeopleSoft Query in Financial Reporting.

CONTENTS

Chapter 1: Introduction to SQL 1

    A.   What is SQL? 1

    B.   Case Study 3

    C.   Table v/s Record 5

    D.   Preliminary SQL Review 6

    E.   Alias & Joins 12

Chapter 2: Introduction to PeopleSoft Query 16

    A.   PeopleSoft Reporting Tools 16

    B.   The Query Development Methodology: 18

Chapter 3: Query Viewer 20

    A.   Introduction 20

    B.   Running a query with Query Viewer 20

Chapter 4: Query Development Steps with Query Manager .23

Chapter 5: Your First Query 25

   A.   Objective 25

   B.   Create your Query – Stage 1 27

   C.   Create your Query – Stage 2 34

Chapter 6: Level Two – It Gets Better 52

   A.   Objective 52

   B.   Create your Query – XX_TRAIN_002 53

Chapter 7: Level Three – Expressions 73

   A.   Objective 73

   B.   Create Query – XX_TRAIN_003 73

   C.   Create Query – XX_TRAIN_004 77

Chapter 8: Sql Review 90

   A.   View SQL page in PeopleSoft Query Manager 90

Chapter 9: Query Transformations 94

Chapter 10: Grant Suite Tables 96

CHAPTER 1: INTRODUCTION TO SQL

A. What is SQL?

What is SQL? Why should you and I care? How does it relate to PeopleSoft Query?

SQL (Structured Query Language) is the backbone of PeopleSoft Query. The PeopleSoft Query Manager creates SQL - "Select" statements as we create a query and allows us to review these SQL statements at any time through a "View SQL" tab. The PeopleSoft Query Viewer and Query Manager run these SQL statements through a "View SQL" tab.

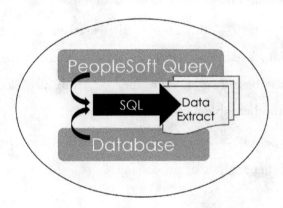

Fig 1.01

SQL is a set of programmatic instructions used to communicate with a database. It is the standard language for

1

relational database management systems.

SQL statements can perform tasks such as inserting data into, updating data in, or extracting data from a database. Most database management systems (DBMS) such as Microsoft SQL Server, Oracle and PostgreSQL use SQL although they have a few unique commands.

The most common SQL commands are "Select", "Insert", "Update" and "Delete".

- "Delete" - this command is used to delete data from a table.

- "Update" - this command is used to change data within one or more fields in a table.

- "Insert" — this command is used to insert new data into a table — either from a source external to the database (e.g. a data file) or from data located in another table within the database.

- "Select" — this is used to extract data for reporting or other analysis or processing.

PeopleSoft Query, being a reporting tool, creates "Select" statements and runs them in order to extract data according to defined specifications.

B. Case Study

For our Case Study, we will use (3) three predefined projects from the PeopleSoft Demo environment. Our task will be to report on these projects.

In PeopleSoft, there are 3 main tables that hold Project data PROJECT (Project Profile Information), PROJ_RESOURCE (Project Transaction information) and CA_DETAIL_PROJ (Project Contract Relationship). In the PeopleSoft database, these tables have a prefix of "PS_".

Sample profile information in table - PS_PROJECT is listed below:

Table 1.01			
Field	**Data Set 1**	**Data Set 2**	**Data Set 3**
BUSINESS_UNIT	EGV05	EGV05	EGV05
PROJECT_ID	PI-PRJ30	PI-PRJ50	PI-PRJ60
EFF_STATUS	A(Active)	A(Active)	A(Active)
PROJECT_TYPE	<blank>	CNSLT	R&D
START_DT	01/01/2007	01/01/2007	01/01/2008
END_DT	12/31/2009	12/31/2011	12/31/2009

PeopleSoft Demo Environment has several transactions for the projects listed above – we will consider a few as listed in the tables below for the table - PROJ_RESOURCE

1) Budget Rows:

Table 1.02			
Field	Data Set 1	Data Set 2	Data Set 3
BUSINESS_UNIT	EGV05	EGV05	EGV05
PROJECT_ID	PI-PRJ30	PI-PRJ50	PI-PRJ50
RESOURCE_ID	10002499	10002509	10002508
ANALYSIS_TYPE	BUD	BUD	BUD
TRANS_DT	08/06/2009	08/06/2009	08/06/2009
RESOURCE_AMOUNT	9,872,000.00	200,000,000.00	400,000,000.00

2) Payables Expense Rows:

Table 1.03			
Field	Data Set 1	Data Set 2	Data Set 3
BUSINESS_UNIT	EGV05	EGV05	EGV05
PROJECT_ID	PI-PRJ30	PI-PRJ50	PI-PRJ50
RESOURCE_ID	10002587	10002590	10002591
ANALYSIS_TYPE	ACT	ACT	ACT
TRANS_DT	01/01/2008	05/02/2007	06/01/2008
RESOURCE_AMOUNT	6,000,000.00	200,000,000.00	400,000,000.00

Sample Project Contract relationship information in table - CA_DETAIL_PROJ is listed below:

Table 1.05			
Field	Data Set 1	Data Set 2	Data Set 3
BUSINESS_UNIT_PC	EGV05	EGV05	EGV05
PROJECT_ID	PI-PRJ30	PI-PRJ50	PI-PRJ60
CONTRACT_NUM	PI-PRP003	PI-PRP005	PI-PRP006

Note: We will use the above tables to take you through PeopleSoft Query.

C. Table v/s Record

Although the term Table and Record are used interchangeably in our day to day working with PeopleSoft, the difference is in whether we are accessing data in PeopleSoft or directly in the database. For the purpose of this book, we will refer to Record when we work with data within PeopleSoft online tools and we will refer to Tables when we directly access data in the database using a SQL tool such as SQL developer or TOAD.

In this book, when we use PeopleSoft tables and records in a

SQL statement, they will have a "PS_" prefix.

D. Preliminary SQL Review

1) Here is the SQL statement that you would write to list out all fields in table PROJECT:

- SELECT * FROM PS_PROJECT;

- SELECT BUSINESS_UNIT, PROJECT_ID, EFF_STATUS, PROJECT_TYPE, START_DT, END_DT FROM PS_PROJECT;

In the above statements,

   a) "SELECT" is the command to extract the data

   b) "*" indicates all fields

   c) "FROM" indicates that this will be followed by the table names

   d) "PS_PROJECT" is the table name.

   e) ";" indicates the end of the statement.

   f) we can use the field list separated by "," in place of "*" if we need specific fields to be extracted

If your database included just the projects listed in table 1.01, your output for Based on our case study, your output for the 2nd SQL statement above will be as listed in table 1.06.

6

Table 1.06			
Field	**Data Set 1**	**Data Set 2**	**Data Set 3**
BUSINESS_UNIT	EGV05	EGV05	EGV05
PROJECT_ID	PI-PRJ30	PI-PRJ50	PI-PRJ60
EFF_STATUS	A(Active)	A(Active)	A(Active)
PROJECT_TYPE	<blank>	CNSLT	R&D
START_DT	01/01/2007	01/01/2007	01/01/2008
END_DT	12/31/2009	12/31/2011	12/31/2009

Similarly, if I needed to extract all fields from the table PS_PROJ_RESOURCE, my SQL statement would be:

- SELECT * FROM PS_PROJ_RESOURCE;

2) Taking this one step further - let's include a "WHERE" clause:

- SELECT BUSINESS_UNIT, PROJECT_ID, EFF_STATUS, PROJECT_TYPE, START_DT, END_DT FROM PS_PROJECT WHERE BUSINESS_UNIT = 'EGV05' AND PROJECT_TYPE = 'CNSLT';

If we run this SQL statement against data in our Case Study, our output will be as below:

Table 1.07	
Field	**Data Set 2**
BUSINESS_UNIT	EGV05
PROJECT_ID	PI-PRJ50
EFF_STATUS	A
PROJECT_TYPE	CNSLT
START_DT	01/01/2007
END_DT	12/31/2011

Note: Rows for PROJECT_ID = PI-PRJ30 and PI-PRJ60 were not extracted since they did not meet the condition – PROJECT_TYPE = 'CNSLT' (Refer to Table 1.01 for the entire group of data sets).

In this SQL statement:

a) "WHERE" signifies that criteria (or conditions) for this extract will follow. Criteria allow us to narrow the data extracted to those that meet specific conditions. For example:

Specifying criteria BUSINESS_UNIT = 'EGV05', will

8

allow us to list data from table PROJECT that only have value 'EGV05' in the field BUSINESS_UNIT.

b) "AND" lists data where both conditions are met - BUSINESS_UNIT = 'EGV05' AND PROJECT_TYPE = 'CNSLT'

3) Now, let us list trim the field list further:

- SELECT PROJECT_ID, EFF_STATUS, PROJECT_TYPE, START_DT, END_DT FROM PS_PROJECT WHERE BUSINESS_UNIT = 'EGV05' AND PROJECT_TYPE = 'CNSLT';

Our Case Study output will list out as below:

Table 1.08	
Field	**Data Set 2**
PROJECT_ID	PI-PRJ50
EFF_STATUS	A
PROJECT_TYPE	CNSLT
START_DT	01/01/2007
END_DT	12/31/2011

Note: BUSINESS_UNIT was not in our list of fields – it will not appear in our extract.

4) Taking the SQL one step further — let's add parentheses and "OR" to our criteria:

- SELECT BUSINESS_UNIT, PROJECT_ID, EFF_STATUS, PROJECT_TYPE, START_DT, END_DT FROM PS_PROJECT WHERE BUSINESS_UNIT='EGV05' AND (PROJECT_TYPE = 'CNSLT' OR START_DT < '2013-JAN-01');

In this example we have added criteria with "AND" & "OR" as conditions. We have also included parentheses.

a) "OR" lists data where either condition is met - PROJECT_TYPE = 'CNSLT' OR START_DT < '2013- JAN-01'

b) "AND" lists data where both conditions are met - BUSINESS_UNIT='EGV05' AND (EFF_STATUS = 'A' OR START_DT < '2013-JAN-01')

c) The parentheses override the priority in which the criteria are processed

Since the condition (PROJECT_TYPE = 'CNSLT' OR

START_DT < '2013-JAN-01') is within parentheses, it will be processed first – resulting in rows being extracted where one of the following two conditions are met (Table 1.09):

i)   (BUSINESS_UNIT='EGV05' AND
        PROJECT_TYPE = 'CNSLT') or

ii)   (BUSINESS_UNIT='EGV05' AND START_DT
        < '2013-JAN-01').

Table 1.09			
Field	Data Set 1	Data Set 2	Data Set 3
BUSINESS_UNIT	EGV05	EGV05	EGV05
PROJECT_ID	PI-PRJ30	PI-PRJ50	PI-PRJ60
EFF_STATUS	A(Active)	A(Active)	A(Active)
PROJECT_TYPE	<blank>	CNSLT	R&D
START_DT	01/01/2007	01/01/2007	01/01/2008
END_DT	12/31/2009	12/31/2011	12/31/2009

Without the parentheses, processing will be in the order in which the statement is written. First – (BUSINESS_UNIT = 'EGV05' AND PROJECT_TYPE = 'CNSLT') and then the result will be processed against (OR START_DT<'2013-JAN-01') to check for rows that meet either condition.

E. Alias & Joins

In SQL, a join is a link between 2 tables on one or more common fields.

In PeopleSoft Query Manager (as we will cover in the next few chapters), we can join 2 or more tables with common fields in one of 2 ways — a standard join or a left outer join.

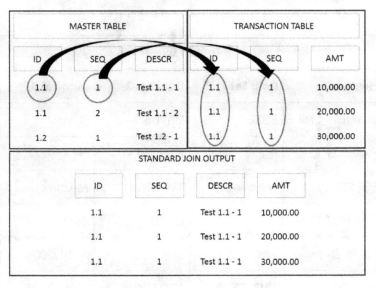

Fig 1.02

A <u>Standard Join</u> extracts all rows that have the same values in the joined fields. In our example, if we join the two tables PS_PROJECT and PS_PROJ_RESOURCE on common fields BUSINESS_UNIT and PROJECT_ID using a standard join, our output will be a list of all rows in those 2 tables with common values in fields BUSINESS_UNIT ('EGV05') and

12

PROJECT_ID (PI-PRJ30, PI-PRJ50, PI-PRJ60).

- SELECT A.PROJECT_ID, A.PROJECT_TYPE,
  B.RESOURCE_ID, B.ANALYSIS_TYPE FROM
  PS_PROJECT A, PS_PROJ_RESOURCE B
  WHERE
  A.BUSINESS_UNIT=B.BUSINESS_UNIT AND
  A.PROJECT_ID=B.PROJECT_ID AND
  A.PROJECT_TYPE<> ' ' AND
  B.ANALYSIS_TYPE='BUD';

In the above statement, I have underscored A and B. These are called aliases. An alias is a word or nickname that we use to represent a table. It shortens the statement and makes it more presentable and manageable.

If I had not used aliases above, the statement would have been as below with the results as in table 1.10:

- SELECT PS_PROJECT.PROJECT_ID,
  PS_PROJECT.PROJECT_TYPE,
  PS_PROJ_RESOURCE.RESOURCE_ID,
  PS_PROJ_RESOURCE.ANALYSIS_TYPE,
  PS_PROJ_RESOURCE.TRANS_DT FROM
  PS_PROJECT, PS_PROJ_RESOURCE WHERE
  PS_PROJECT.BUSINESS_UNIT =
  PS_PROJ_RESOURCE.BUSINESS_UNIT AND

PS_PROJECT.PROJECT_ID=

PS_PROJ_RESOURCE.PROJECT_ID AND

PS_PROJECT.PROJECT_TYPE<> ' ' AND

PS_PROJ_RESOURCE.ANALYSIS_TYPE='BUD';

Table 1.10				
PROJECT_ ID	PROJECT _TYPE	RESOURCE_ ID	ANALYSIS_ TYPE	RESOURCE_ AMOUNT
PI-PRJ50	CNSLT	10002509	BUD	200,000,000.00
PI-PRJ50	CNSLT	10002508	BUD	400,000,000.00

Since PI-PRJ60 has no transactions in PROJ_RESOURCE for ANALYSIS_TYPE='BUD', it is not generated in the output.

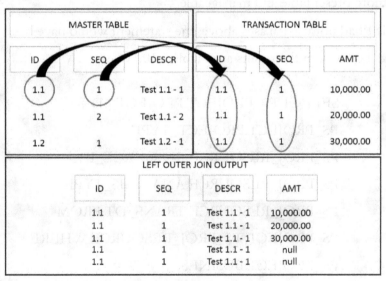

Fig 1.03

14

A <u>Left Outer Join</u> extracts all rows from the first table and rows from the 2nd table that have the same values as that of the first table in the joined fields. In addition to this we can add criteria to trim-down the output as in the statement below.

- SELECT A.PROJECT_ID, A.PROJECT_TYPE, B.RESOURCE_ID, B.ANALYSIS_TYPE FROM PS_PROJECT A LEFT OUTER JOIN PS_PROJ_RESOURCE B ON A.BUSINESS_UNIT=B.BUSINESS_UNIT AND A.PROJECT_ID=B.PROJECT_ID WHERE A.PROJECT_TYPE<> ' ' AND B.ANALYSIS_TYPE='BUD';

Table 1.11				
PROJECT_ ID	PROJECT _TYPE	RESOURCE_ ID	ANALYSIS_ TYPE	RESOURCE_ AMOUNT
PI-PRJ50	CNSLT	10002509	BUD	200,000,000.00
PI-PRJ50	CNSLT	10002508	BUD	400,000,000.00
PI-PRJ60	CNSLT	null	null	null

Chapter 2: Introduction to PeopleSoft Query

A. PeopleSoft Reporting Tools

1) PeopleSoft Query: This is a tool that generates SQL select statements to extract data from one or more PeopleSoft tables. This tool is also used in other reporting tools and PeopleSoft workflow.

2) PeopleSoft nVision: This is a reporting tool that generates its output into excel spreadsheets. This provides users with the flexibility to use excel formulas in their reports for further analysis.

3) Crystal Reports for PeopleSoft: Crystal Reports is owned by SAP. It allows users to graphically define data relationships. Users create a report layout. Users can select and link tables from a wide variety of data sources, including PeopleSoft query.

4) PeopleSoft BI Publisher: This reporting tool uses Microsoft Word or any other rich text editor to create a report layout. Code can be inserted into the document and data is fed into the layout from

PeopleSoft query or other data sources.

5) SQR for PeopleSoft: SQR is a programming language which is used to process data in PeopleSoft. SQR is also used for reporting. The advantages of using SQR for reporting are:

- It is flexible - being a program, code can be written to produce data in any form (csv, pdf, etc.).

- It can be used to process high volumes of data while reporting in the same process.

- It can work across platforms. Data can be processed and reported on, from multiple environments in the same report.

6) Pivot Grid: Pivot grids enable users to analyze data extracted using PeopleSoft Query resulting in multiple dimensions for the same data. It generates charts and graphs which get refreshed as the data changes. This saves the user the trouble involved in exporting the data to excel and creating pivot tables and managing excel files with that data.

7) In addition to the above, PeopleSoft provides Interactive reports. These are online pages available as part of each module, to extract data online, based on

online parameters. The User selects values for the parameters and these are used to select data from the PeopleSoft tables.

8) Other non-PeopleSoft tools are TOAD SQL tool and Oracle SQL developer. Both of these are used to process data as well as extract data into excel spreadsheets. These are programming tools that run SQL commands and are used by developers and experienced analysts.

B. The Query Development Methodology:

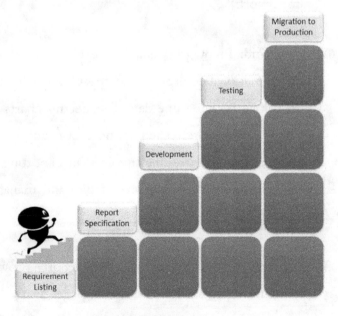

Fig 2.01

1) List out the requirement in an issue log or a reporting log

2) Create a Report Specification after review of the log to ensure that the query does not already exist.

3) Develop and test the query in a reporting environment. Alternately, you may develop the query in the reporting environment and migrate it to the test environment.

4) Test the query using scenarios listed in your specification.

5) Migrate the query to Production.

Chapter 3: Query Viewer

A. Introduction

PeopleSoft Query Viewer is used to extract data using pre-defined queries. As the name suggests, this feature of PeopleSoft Query will allow the user to view the data online or to download it into excel spreadsheet or an xml file.

B. Running a query with Query Viewer

Step 01.   Navigation

Using the navigation in the picture (Fig 3.01).

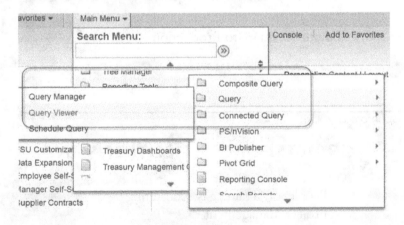

Fig 3.01

Step 02.   Query Search

Enter part of a Query Name click on Search (Fig 3.02).

Fig 3.02

Step 03.   Output Options

Click on one of the output options — HTML, Excel, or XML (Fig 3.03).

Fig 3.03

If there are prompt values in the query i.e. if the query requires the user to enter some information before extracting the data (Fig 3.04), populate values for the prompted fields and click on the **"View Results"** button.

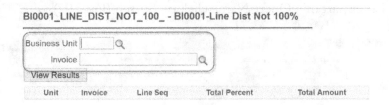

Fig 3.04

If the "Excel" or "XML" output option was selected, a file download pop-up will appear as in Fig 3.05

Fig 3.05

CHAPTER 4: QUERY DEVELOPMENT STEPS WITH QUERY MANAGER

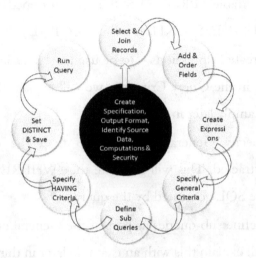

Fig 4.01

Below are the list of steps involved in development of a query. In the next three chapters, we will use them in examples.

1) Navigate to Query Manager

2) Select records – join records where the extract is from more than one record (for example, select records PROJECT and PROJ_RESOURCE – Standard join on fields BUSINESS_UNIT and PROJECT_ID)

3) Select Fields for the extract.

   a) Select the Order of Field display for the query

   b) Select the sort order for the query (This generates the "ORDER BY" clause in SQL).

c) Setup Aggregate fields where applicable (This lets you find the total for a group of fields – for example if we need to find the sum of RESOURCE_AMOUNT in table PROJ_RESOURCE grouped by fields BUSINESS_UNIT and PROJECT_ID)

4) Create Expressions – to be used as Fields in the Query or in the Query Criteria – we will explain this with an example later in this book.

5) Specify General criteria – to filter the data being extracted. This will generate the "WHERE" clause of the SQL generated by the query.

6) Define sub-queries as part of the General criteria – we will explain this with an example later in this book.

7) Specify "having" criteria for aggregate fields. The "HAVING" clause is similar to the "WHERE" clause – it filters the extract based on the aggregate fields (for example – Select project_id, sum(resource_amount) from ps_proj_resource where business_unit='EGV05' **having sum(resource_amount) > 20000** group by project_id.

8) Save the query with or without the "distinct" flag.

Chapter 5: Your First Query

A. Objective

The objective of this chapter is to:

a) create a Query with tables:

- PROJECT

- PROJ_RESOURCE

b) Select Fields:

- PROJECT_ID

- PROJECT_TYPE

- RESOURCE_ID

- ANALYSIS_TYPE

- RESOURCE_AMOUNT

c) Setup criteria to narrow down the output.

- BUSINESS_UNIT = 'EGV05'

- PROJECT_ID in list ('PI-PRJ30','PI-PRJ50', 'PI-PRJ60')

- PROJECT_TYPE='CNSLT'

d) Save the Query:

- As a public query – XX_TRAIN_001

e) Run this query to extract data as below:

Table 5.01				
PROJECT_ID	**PROJECT_TYPE**	**RESOURCE_ID**	**ANALYSIS_TYPE**	**RESOURCE_AMOUNT**
PI-PRJ50	CNSLT	10002504	BUD	1,000,000.00
PI-PRJ50	CNSLT	10002505	BUD	200,000,000.00
PI-PRJ50	CNSLT	10002506	BUD	100,000,000.00
PI-PRJ50	CNSLT	10002507	BUD	2,000,000.00
PI-PRJ50	CNSLT	10002508	BUD	400,000,000.00
PI-PRJ50	CNSLT	10002509	BUD	200,000,000.00
PI-PRJ50	CNSLT	10002510	BUD	4,000,000.00
PI-PRJ50	CNSLT	10002511	BUD	800,000,000.00
PI-PRJ50	CNSLT	10002512	BUD	400,000,000.00
PI-PRJ50	CNSLT	10002513	BUD	8,000,000.00
PI-PRJ50	CNSLT	10002514	BUD	1,600,000,000.00
PI-PRJ50	CNSLT	10002515	BUD	800,000,000.00
PI-PRJ50	CNSLT	10002516	BUD	1,000,000.00
PI-PRJ50	CNSLT	10002517	BUD	200,000,000.00
PI-PRJ50	CNSLT	10002518	BUD	300,000,000.00
PI-PRJ50	CNSLT	10002590	ACT	200,000,000.00
PI-PRJ50	CNSLT	10002591	ACT	400,000,000.00
PI-PRJ50	CNSLT	10002593	BLD	200,000,000.00
PI-PRJ50	CNSLT	10002594	BLD	400,000,000.00
PI-PRJ50	CNSLT	10002605	BIL	200,000,000.00
PI-PRJ50	CNSLT	10002606	BIL	1,000,000.00
PI-PRJ50	CNSLT	PEGV05PI-PO051#1#1DST1	COM	400,000,000.00
PI-PRJ50	CNSLT	REGV05PI-RQ051#1#1#1	REQ	400,000,000.00
PI-PRJ50	CNSLT	REGV05PI-RQ052#1#1#1	REQ	7,624,402.15
PI-PRJ50	CNSLT	VEGV05PI-VCR501 0 1 9627 0	ACT	200,000,000.00
PI-PRJ50	CNSLT	VEGV05PI-VCR502 0 1 9627 0	ACT	1,000,000.00

B. Create your Query – Stage 1

Step 01.   Navigation.

- Navigate to PeopleSoft Query Manager using the navigation in the picture below (Fig. 5.01).

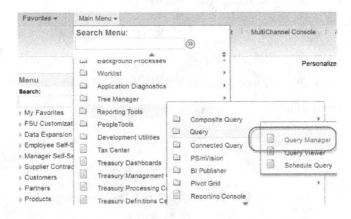

Fig 5.01

- Click on Create New Query hyperlink (Fig. 5.02).

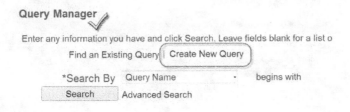

Fig 5.02

- You will be transferred to the "Records" page (Fig 5.03).

Step 02.   Record Selection.

- To proceed with this step, confirm that you are at the "Records" page (Fig 5.03). If you are not at the "Records" page, go back and repeat the previous step.

- Enter the name (or part of the name) of the record you intend to use for your query. This is marked with a red box against a red "A" in Fig 5.03. In this example, we will enter "PROJECT" as the record name.

- Click on the "Search" button. This is marked with a red box against a red "B" in Fig 5.03.

- You get a list of records that have a name that start with the name you have provided. This is marked with a red box against a red "C" in Fig 5.03.

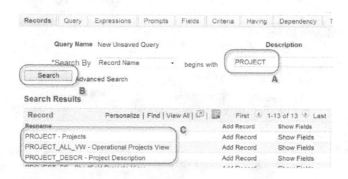

Fig 5.03

- You can also search by other parameters (as in the Fig 5.04 below)

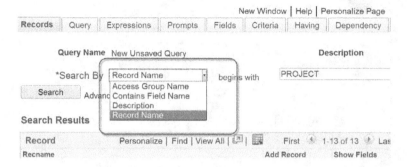

Fig 5.04

- Click on the Add Record hyperlink against the record PROJECT. You can click on the Show Fields hyperlink to look at all the fields of this record before adding the record to the query (Fig 5.05).

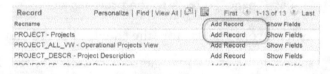

Fig 5.05

- You will get transferred to the "Query" page. This page lists out the selected tables and all their fields.

Step 03.   Field Selection.

Fig 5.06

- To proceed with this step, confirm that you are at the "Query" page (Fig 5.06). If you are not at the "Query" page, go back to the previous step.

- Select your fields for the query by individually selecting the checkbox against each field desired. For our case study, select 2 fields — PROJECT_ID and PROJECT_TYPE.

- Other features on this page that assist in field selection:

  i. "Check All" button - to select all fields.

  ii. First/Last hyperlinks – to get to the first field or Last field (as applicable)

  iii. ⊲ or ⊳ - to make visible the next set of fields before or after (as applicable) the current set.

  iv. ⊟ - collapses the field list for a record.

Step 04.   Saving the Query

Why am I saving the Query now? Why am I not going through the entire query development cycle and then saving the query?

As with every other application and tool in PeopleSoft, the Query Manager can shut down at any time for reasons that we have all experienced at some point:

a) Timing-out of your PeopleSoft instance.

b) Problems with your computer - your internet connection, VPN connection or browser.

To save us the heartache of losing the query and having to create it again, you should save your query often.

- Scroll to the bottom of the page and click on the "Save" button. A page as in Fig 5.06a will emerge.

Enter a name to save this query:

*Query	
Description	
Folder	
*Query Type	User
*Owner	Private

Query Definition:

| OK | Cancel |

Fig 5.07

31

- Enter the detail as below for each field:

  i.   Query – Enter a name for the Query – XX_TRAIN_001 (Replace 'XX' with your initials to allow others using the same PeopleSoft environment to make use of this book).

  ii. Description – Enter a short Description about this Query. The description should provide a clear understanding of the purpose of this query in order to let others use it in the future.

  iii. Query Type – Leave as "User". Refer to table 5.02 for a list of Query types and their purposes.

  iv. Owner – Leave this value as "Public". A Public Query can be accessed by all users. A Private Query can be accessed by the person creating it.

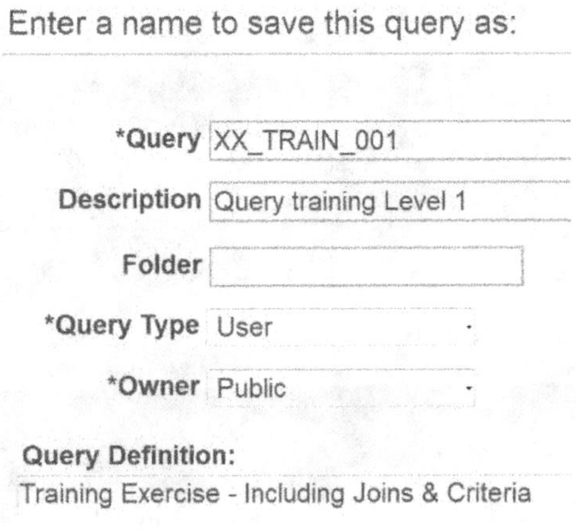

Enter a name to save this query as:

*Query	XX_TRAIN_001
Description	Query training Level 1
Folder	
*Query Type	User
*Owner	Public

Query Definition:

Training Exercise - Including Joins & Criteria

Fig 5.08

- Click on "OK" to Save

Table 5.02

It is important to understand the different types of Queries before going to the next step in our case study.

❖ <u>User Queries:</u> These are Queries designed and run from PeopleSoft Query Manager, Query Viewer or the Query Designer tool provided with the PeopleSoft Application Designer. These include Reporting Queries used by PeopleSoft and External Reporting tools such as Crystal Reports, nVision, Cube Manager and BI Publisher.

❖ <u>Process Queries:</u> These are queries that are run periodically in a batch process.

❖ <u>Role Query:</u> These are queries created specifically for PeopleSoft Workflow. They return a list of role. This query joins the record PSROLEUSER or ROLEXLATOPR with other records to provide a role user list based on conditions required for the workflow design. These are saved with names that begin with [ROLE] in order to identify them distinctly as role queries.

❖ <u>Archive Query:</u> This is a query that is used by PeopleSoft Data Archive Manager for archiving.

C. Create your Query – Stage 2

In this stage we will:

- Add record PROJ_RESOURCE with a "Standard Join"
- Select fields from PROJ_RESOURCE
- Add Criteria – to filter the data
- Save and Run the Query

Step 01.   Record Join.

- Click on the "Records" tab — this will take you to the "Records" page. This is marked with a red box against a red "A" in Fig 5.09

- Enter the name (or part of the name) of the record you intend to use for your query. This is marked with a red box against a red "B" in Fig 5.09. In this example, we will enter "PROJ_RESOURCE" as the record name.

- Click on the "Search" button. This is marked with a red box against a red "C" in Fig 5.09.

- You get a list of records that have a name that start with the name you have provided.

34

- Click on the "Join Record" hyperlink. This is marked with a red box against a red "D" in Fig 5.09.

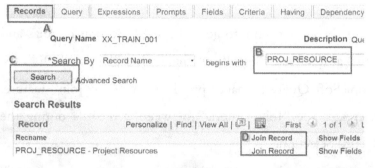

Fig 5.09

- You will be taken to the screen displayed in Fig 5.10 to select the type of join and the record to join with.

- Select the join type and the join record from the list. For our example:

i. Select the radio button against "Join to filter and get additional fields (Standard Join)" and

ii. Click on A=PROJECT — Projects hyperlink.

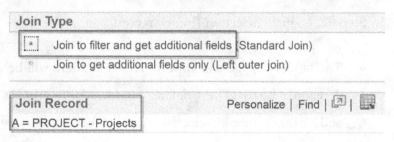

Fig 5.10

- On clicking the A=PROJECT — Projects hyperlink the Auto Join Criteria page will appear.

This is be a good time to go to Page 12 (Section E. Alias and Joins) and refresh yourself on what a "Join" does in SQL".

PeopleSoft Query Manager provides an "Auto Join" feature. It creates the "Join Criteria" between 2 records during the Record Selection.

Now that you have an understanding about Joins, we will continue with our exercise:

- Click on the "Add Criteria" button (Fig 5.11).

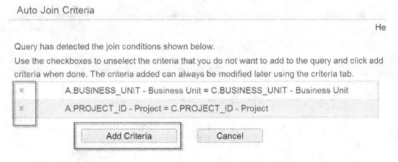

Auto Join Criteria

He

Query has detected the join conditions shown below.
Use the checkboxes to unselect the criteria that you do not want to add to the query and click add criteria when done. The criteria added can always be modified later using the criteria tab.

| ☑ | A.BUSINESS_UNIT - Business Unit = C.BUSINESS_UNIT - Business Unit |
| ☑ | A.PROJECT_ID - Project = C.PROJECT_ID - Project |

Add Criteria   Cancel

Fig 5.11

Step 02.   Field Selection (Joined record).

- The "Query" page will appear. This time there will be 2 records listed (The original record - A.PROJECT and the one selected for the join - B.PROJ_RESOURCE). Note the "Alias" prefixed to each record.

- Select fields from the second record that need to be displayed in the query output by checking the checkbox next to the field. In our example,

  i. Select RESOURCE_ID, JOURNAL_ID and ANALYSIS_TYPE.

  ii. Click on the "Find" hyperlink in Fig 5.12b. A pop-up appears as in Fig. 5.12a.

  iii. Enter "RESOURCE_AMOUNT" and click on "OK". The list in record PROJ_RESOURCE changes with RESOURCE_AMOUNT at the top of the list (Fig. 5.12b).

  iv. Check the box against RESOURCE_AMOUNT

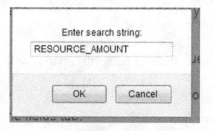

Fig 5.12b

- To collapse the field list for PROJ_RESOURCE, click on the folder icon against the PROJ_RESOURCE table as in the picture below.

  B PROJ_RESOURCE - Project Resources

- Click on the "Save" button.

Step 03.   Order, Sort & Delete Fields

- Click on the "Fields" tab (Fig. 5.13). You will see the fields added to the query in the earlier steps.

- This page in Query manager allows us to re-order sort and delete fields selected in a query.

- Click on the Reorder/Sort button (Fig. 5.13).

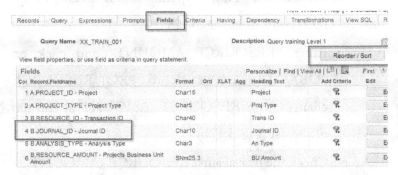

Fig 5.13

- The "Edit Field Ordering" page will appear (Fig. 5.14).

- To re-order columns, enter the desired column number in the "New Column" field. In our example, we will move field JOURNAL_ID to column 6 by entering 6 in the "New Column" field (Fig. 5.14).

- To Sort the data by a field value, enter the order number in the "New Order By" field.

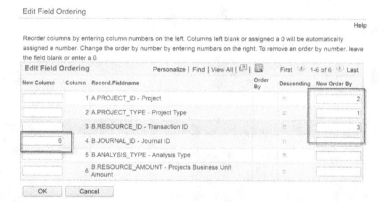

Reorder columns by entering column numbers on the left. Columns left blank or assigned a 0 will be automatically assigned a number. Change the order by number by entering numbers on the right. To remove an order by number, leave the field blank or enter a 0.

Fig 5.14

- Click on "OK". You will be taken to the "Fields" page again. This time, in our example, you will see the field JOURNAL_ID as the 6th field (Fig. 5.15). You will also notice the Sort Order in the "ORD" column of the grid.

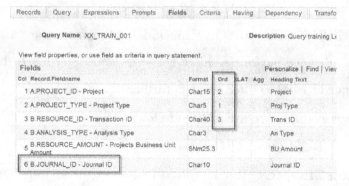

Fig 5.15

- To delete a field from the query, click on the ⊟ icon at the far right of name of the field name that needs to

be deleted. In our example we will delete
JOURNAL_ID.

- Note that in Fig. 5.16, the 6th field is missing.

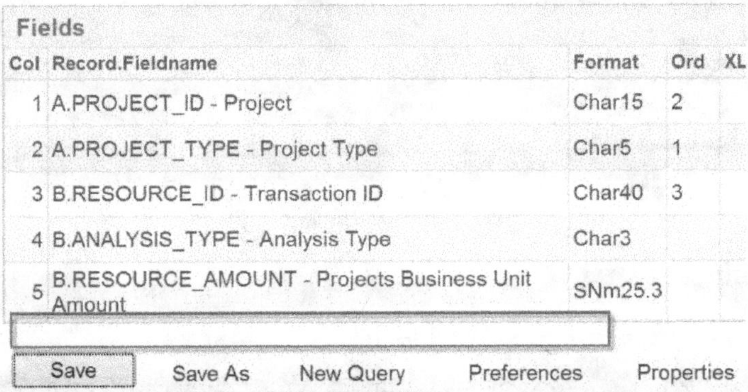

Fields				
Col	Record.Fieldname	Format	Ord	XL
1	A.PROJECT_ID - Project	Char15	2	
2	A.PROJECT_TYPE - Project Type	Char5	1	
3	B.RESOURCE_ID - Transaction ID	Char40	3	
4	B.ANALYSIS_TYPE - Analysis Type	Char3		
5	B.RESOURCE_AMOUNT - Projects Business Unit Amount	SNm25.3		

Save   Save As   New Query   Preferences   Properties

Fig 5.16

- Save your query.

Step 04.   Add Criteria

"Criteria" in Query Manager is the setup that creates the
"WHERE" clause in SQL. It includes setup from the "Auto
Join" that we performed in earlier steps and other items that
we need to add to filter our data further.

In our example, we will add the following criteria

a) BUSINESS_UNIT = 'EGV05'

b) PROJECT_ID in list ('PI-PRJ30','PI-PRJ50', 'PI-
PRJ60')

c) PROJECT_TYPE='CNSLT'

After we set up the above criteria, I will provide an

explanation of the different types of criteria that can be added in a query.

- Click on the "Criteria" tab. The "Criteria" page will appear (Fig 5.17). You will see 2 criteria existing already. These were set up by the Auto Join between records PROJECT and PROJ_RESOURCE.

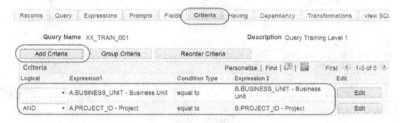

Fig 5.17

- Click on the "Add Criteria" button (Fig 5.17). The "Edit Criteria Properties" page appears (Fig 5.18).

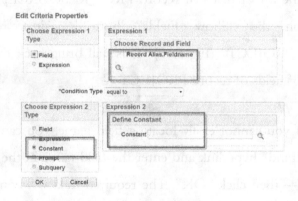

Fig 5.18

- Click on the 🔍 icon below "Record Alias.Fieldname" (Fig 5.18). The "Select a Field" page appears (Fig with

the Record names and the list of fields of the 1st
Record (Fig 5.19).

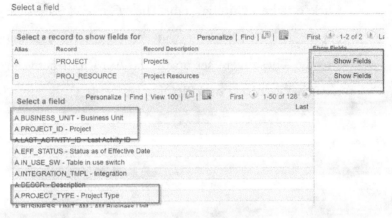

Fig 5.19

- Click on the "Show Fields" button against record
  "PROJ_RESOURCE" (Fig 5.19). This will bring up
  the list of fields of record PROJ_RESOURCE. Click
  on the "Show Fields" button against record
  "PROJECT" (Fig 5.19). This will bring back the list
  of fields of record PROJECT.

Note: If you cannot easily locate a field name, you can click
on the "Find" hyperlink and enter the field name in the pop-
up box — then click "OK". The required field will come up
as the first field on the list of fields.

- Click on "A.BUSINESS_UNIT" from the list. The
  pop-up page disappears and takes you back to the

"Edit Criteria Properties" page. At this point you should note that A.BUSINESS_UNIT now appears below the label "Record Alias.Fieldname" (Fig 5.20a).

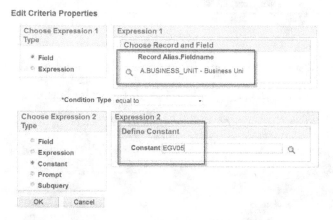

Fig 5.20a

- The next step is selection of a Condition Type. For our current criteria, we will select "equal to".

- The options in the "Choose Expression 2 Type" group box changes with change in Condition Type. For our current criteria, we will leave the selection as it appears in Fig 5.20a - "Constant".

- Enter "EGV05" in the "Constant" field and click on the "OK" button.

- Click on the "OK" button — the "Criteria" page appears again with a row added (Fig. 5.20b).

- Save your query.

Criteria			Personalize | Find | 🗐 | 🖼 F
Logical	Expression1	Condition Type	Expression 2
	• A.BUSINESS_UNIT - Business Unit	equal to	B.BUSINESS_UNIT - Business Unit
AND	• A.PROJECT_ID - Project	equal to	B.PROJECT_ID - Project
AND	• A.BUSINESS_UNIT - Business Unit	equal to	EGV05

Fig 5.20b

- Repeat the above bullet points in this step for field A.PROJECT_TYPE="CNSLT". The criteria page after this criteria will look as in Fig 5.21.

Query Name XX_TRAIN_001   **Description** Quer

Add Criteria		Group Criteria		Reorder Criteria	

Criteria			Personalize | Find | 🗐 |
Logical	Expression1	Condition Type	Expression 2
	• A.BUSINESS_UNIT - Business Unit	equal to	B.BUSINESS_UNIT - B Unit
AND	• A.PROJECT_ID - Project	equal to	B.PROJECT_ID - Proje
AND	• A.BUSINESS_UNIT - Business Unit	equal to	EGV05
AND	• A.PROJECT_TYPE - Project Type	equal to	CNSLT

Fig 5.21

We will now add a different criteria type – "In List". We will use this to filter the data by a specific list of Project IDs - ('PI-PRJ30','PI-PRJ50', 'PI-PRJ60')

- Click on the "Add Criteria" button (Fig 5.21). The "Edit Criteria Properties" page appears (Fig 5.18).

- In the Expression 1 group box, select PROJECT_ID following the steps taken in setting up the previous 2 criteria

- The next step is selection of a Condition Type. For

our case study, we will select "in List".

- The options in the "Choose Expression 2 Type" box change with the default selection as "in List". We now have 2 options: "In List" and "Subquery" (Fig 5.22).

Edit Criteria Properties

Choose Expression 1 Type	Expression 1
⦿ Field	Choose Record and Field
○ Expression	Record Alias.Fieldname
	🔍 A.PROJECT_ID - Project

*Condition Type: in list

Choose Expression 2 Type	Expression 2
⦿ In List	Edit List
○ Subquery	List Members 🔍

OK   Cancel

Fig 5.22

- Click on the 🔍 icon in the "Expression 2" box. The "Edit List" page appears (Fig 5.23a).

Edit List   ✖

Help

No values have been added yet.

Value: [＿＿＿＿＿＿＿＿＿]   Add Value   Search

Add Prompt

OK   Cancel

Fig 5.23a

- Enter "PI-PRJ30" in the "Value" field and click on the "Add Value" button (Fig 5.23a). You will now see

"PI-PRJ30" in the "List of Members" box. Repeat for "PI-PRJ50", and "PI-PRJ30" and then click "OK" (Fig 5.23b).

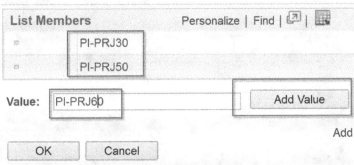

Fig 5.23b

- You will see these values in the "Edit Criteria Properties" page - "List of Members" box (Fig 5.24).

Edit Criteria Properties

Choose Expression 1 Type	Expression 1
* Field	Choose Record and Field
Expression	Record Alias.Fieldname
	Q A.PROJECT_ID - Project

*Condition Type in list

Choose Expression 2 Type	Expression 2
* In List	Edit List
Subquery	List Members ('PI-PRJ30','PI-PRJ50','PI-PRJ60') Q

Fig 5.24

- Click on the "OK" button — the "Criteria" page appears again with a row added (Fig 5.25).

46

Criteria			Personalize | Find | 🖳 | 🖩	FI
Logical	Expression1	Condition Type	Expression 2	
	• A.BUSINESS_UNIT - Business Unit	equal to	B.BUSINESS_UNIT - Business Unit	
AND	• A.PROJECT_ID - Project	equal to	B.PROJECT_ID - Project	
AND	• A.BUSINESS_UNIT - Business Unit	equal to	EGV05	
AND	• A.PROJECT_TYPE - Project Type	equal to	CNSLT	
AND	• A.PROJECT_ID - Project	in list	('PI-PRJ30','PI-PRJ50','PI-PRJ60')	

Fig 5.25

- Save your query.

Table 5.03

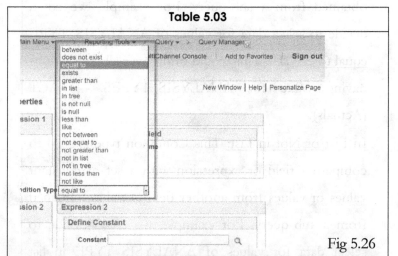

Fig 5.26

Now, let us understand Condition Types. In the "Edit Criteria Properties" page above, we see 18 Condition Types. These condition types determine the type of "WHERE" clause that will result from this criteria setup.

a) <u>Between or Not Between:</u> This is used to select data between (and including) 2 specified values. For example, we could decide to select data for values of ANALYSIS_TYPE between "AAA" and "CCC". This would bring over all transactions having values for ANALYSIS_TYPES such as — ACT (Actuals) and BUD (Budgets).

b) <u>Equal to or not equal to, Greater than or not Greater than, Less Than or Not Less Than:</u> This Condition type is used to compare a field or expression with a constant value or a value from another field or a value obtained from a sub-query. For example, we could decide to select data for values of ANALYSIS_TYPE <u>equal to</u> "ACT". This would bring over all transactions having value for ANALYSIS_TYPES — ACT (Actuals).

c) <u>In List or Not in List:</u> This Condition type is used to compare a field or expression with a set of constant values or values from another field or values obtained from a sub-query. For example, we could decide to select data for values of ANALYSIS_TYPE in list "ACT, BUD, GLE, PAY, SFA". This would bring over all transactions having values for ANALYSIS_TYPES in that list.

d) <u>Is Null or Is Not Null:</u> This Condition type is used to check whether a field has a null value. You would use these in most cases to check Date fields and to check fields in a left outer join.

e) <u>Exists or Does not Exist:</u> These are used in Subqueries. Here the condition checks whether the result of another query provides a "TRUE" or "FALSE" condition (as applicable). We will cover subqueries in the next chapter.

f) <u>In Tree or Not in Tree:</u> These condition types filter the data to a set of values within a tree node

- that is specified in the criteria or

- is identified during runtime by selecting a "tree prompt" option in the Edit Criteria Properties" page.

g) <u>Like or Not Like:</u> These condition types allow you to enter a partial value with a ""%" for the missing portion.

For example, use "%PROJ%" to find a list of all values with "PROJ" in them.

Step 05.   Run your Query

You have reached the final stage of your query development cycle for this query – you can run it and observe the results.

- Click on the "Run" tab - the "Run" page appears with your result (Fig 5.27).

49

	Project	Proj Type	Trans ID		An Type	BU Amount
1	PI-PRJ50	CNSLT	10002504		BUD	1000000.00(
2	PI-PRJ50	CNSLT	10002505		BUD	200000000.00(
3	PI-PRJ50	CNSLT	10002506		BUD	100000000.00(
4	PI-PRJ50	CNSLT	10002507		BUD	2000000.00(
5	PI-PRJ50	CNSLT	10002508		BUD	400000000.00(
6	PI-PRJ50	CNSLT	10002509		BUD	200000000.00(
7	PI-PRJ50	CNSLT	10002510		BUD	4000000.00(
8	PI-PRJ50	CNSLT	10002511		BUD	800000000.00(
9	PI-PRJ50	CNSLT	10002512		BUD	400000000.00(
10	PI-PRJ50	CNSLT	10002513		BUD	8000000.00(

Fig 5.27

- You will notice that:

    i. The data is filtered to BUSINESS_UNIT = 'EGV05' and 'PROJECT_TYPE='CNSLT'

    ii. The data is sorted by PROJECT_TYPE, PROJECT_ID and RESOURCE_ID.

- You can rerun the query by clicking on the hyperlink "Rerun Query"

- You can download to Excel by clicking on "Download to Excel" (Fig 5.28 & 5.29).

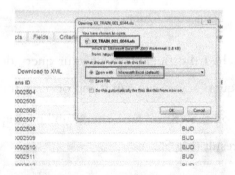

Fig 5.28

50

`A5` `fx` PI-PRJ50

	A	B	C	D	E
1	XX_TRAIN_001	26			
2	Project	Proj Type	Trans ID	An Type	BU Amount
3	PI-PRJ50	CNSLT	10002504	BUD	1000000.000
4	PI-PRJ50	CNSLT	10002505	BUD	200000000.000
5	PI-PRJ50	CNSLT	10002506	BUD	100000000.000
6	PI-PRJ50	CNSLT	10002507	BUD	2000000.000
7	PI-PRJ50	CNSLT	10002508	BUD	400000000.000
8	PI-PRJ50	CNSLT	10002509	BUD	200000000.000
9	PI-PRJ50	CNSLT	10002510	BUD	4000000.000

Fig 5.29

Chapter 6: Level Two – It Gets Better

A. Objective

The objective of this chapter is to:

a) create a Query with tables:

- PROJECT
- PROJ_RESOURCE

b) Select Fields:

- PROJECT_ID
- PROJECT_TYPE
- ANALYSIS_TYPE
- COUNT(RESOURCE_ID) (Number of rows)
- SUM(RESOURCE_AMOUNT) (Total Amount)

c) Criteria to narrow down the output.

- BUSINESS_UNIT = 'EGV05'
- PROJECT_ID in list ('PI-PRJ30','PI-PRJ50', 'PI-PRJ60')
- Subquery with CA_DETAIL_PROJ

d) Add a "HAVING" clause:

- COUNT(BUSINESS_UNIT) >1

e) Run this query to extract data as below:

Table 6.01				
PROJECT _ID	PROJECT_ TYPE	ANALYSIS _TYPE	COUNT (RESOURCE_ID)	SUM (RESOURCE _ AMOUNT)
PI-PRJ30		BUD	9	44,312,000.00
PI-PRJ30		CBU	6	22,808,000.00
PI-PRJ30		CCO	2	186,000.00
PI-PRJ30		CRQ	2	186,000.00
PI-PRJ30		REQ	4	33,960.00
PI-PRJ50	CNSLT	REQ	2	407,624,402.15
PI-PRJ50	CNSLT	BUD	15	5,016,000,000.00
PI-PRJ50	CNSLT	ACT	4	801,000,000.00
PI-PRJ50	CNSLT	BIL	2	201,000,000.00
PI-PRJ50	CNSLT	BLD	2	600,000,000.00
PI-PRJ60	R&D	BIL	2	528,000.00
PI-PRJ60	R&D	BUD	6	1,156,000.00

B. Create your Query – XX_TRAIN_002

Step 01.   Copy Query.

- Navigate to PeopleSoft Query Manager using the navigation in the picture - Fig. 6.01.

- Enter XX (Or your initials) in the search field shown in Fig. 6.01.

- Click on the "Search" button. The Query "XX_TRAIN_001" will appear in the list (Fig. 6.01).

- Click on "Edit"

Query Manager

Enter any information you have and click Search. Leave fields blank for a list of all values.
Find an Existing Query | Create New Query

*Search By   Query Name   ▾   begins with   XX

[Search]   Advanced Search

Search Results

*Folder View   -- All Folders --   ▾

[Check All]   [Uncheck All]   *Action -- Choose -

Query				
Select	Query Name	Descr	Owner	Folde
☑	XX_TRAIN_001	Query training Level 1	Public	

Fig 6.01

- You will be transferred to the "Fields" page (Fig 6.02).

2 A.PROJECT_TYPE - Project Type	Char5	1
3 B.RESOURCE_ID - Transaction ID	Char40	3
4 B.ANALYSIS_TYPE - Analysis Type	Char3	
5 B.RESOURCE_AMOUNT - Projects Business Unit Amount	SNm25.3	

[Save]   [Save As]   New Query   Preferences   Properties

[Return To Search]

Fig 6.02

Enter a name to save this query as:

*Query   XX_TRAIN_001

Description   Query training Level 1

Folder

*Query Type   User

*Owner   Public

Query Definition:
Training Exercise - Including Joins & Criteria   Fig 6.03

54

- Click on "Save As". A pop-up appears as in Fig 6.03.

- Populate the values as in Fig 6.04 and click on "OK".

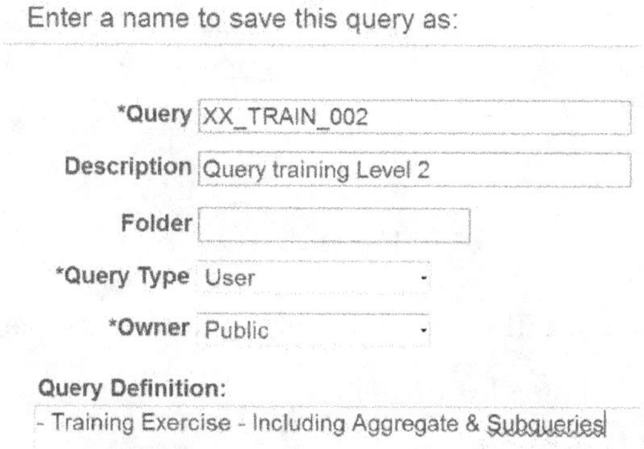

Enter a name to save this query as:

*Query	XX_TRAIN_002
Description	Query training Level 2
Folder	
*Query Type	User
*Owner	Public

Query Definition:
- Training Exercise - Including Aggregate & Subqueries

Fig 6.04

- The Query is saved as XX_TRAIN_002

Step 02.   Aggregate.

This feature of Query manager allows us to aggregate values. We will be able to

a) Summarize or find an average in an amount field (in our example – B.RESOURCE_AMOUNT),

b) Run a count of transaction with a specific combination (in our example – B.RESOURCE_ID),

c) Identify the maximum or minimum value in a field for a specific combination (for example to find the latest date that transactions of a specific type has incurred)

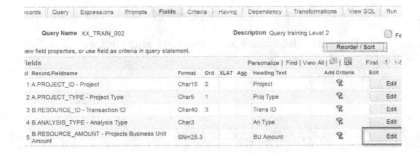

Query Name XX_TRAIN_002   Description Query training Level 2   Fe

iew field properties, or use field as criteria in query statement.   Reorder / Sort

:ields   Personalize | Find | View All | 🖾 | 🖾 First 1-5

ol	Record.Fieldname	Format	Ord	XLAT	Agg	Heading Text	Add Criteria	Edit
1	A.PROJECT_ID - Project	Char15	2			Project	🔍	Edit
2	A.PROJECT_TYPE - Project Type	Char5	1			Proj Type	🔍	Edit
3	B.RESOURCE_ID - Transaction ID	Char40	3			Trans ID	🔍	Edit
4	B.ANALYSIS_TYPE - Analysis Type	Char3				An Type	🔍	Edit
5	B.RESOURCE_AMOUNT - Projects Business Unit Amount	SNm25.3				BU Amount	🔍	Edit

Fig 6.05

- Click on the "Fields" tab. The Fields page appears providing a list of fields

- Click on the "Edit" button as in Fig 6.05 - against field B.RESOURCE_AMOUNT.

- You will be taken to the "Edit Field Properties" page — Fig 6.06a.

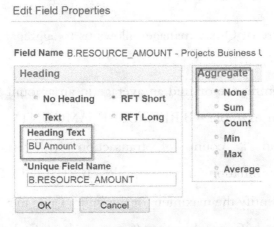

Fig 6.06a

- In the Heading group box, select "Text" and enter a value in the "Heading Text" field (Fig 6.06b). In our example, we will click on the "Text" radio button and enter "Total Amount" in that field in place of "BU Amount".

- In the Aggregate group box, select the option applicable (Fig 6.06b). In our example, we will select "Sum".

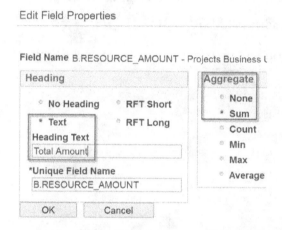

Fig 6.06b

- Click on "OK". You will be taken to the "Fields" page again. This time, in our example, you will see "Sum" in the "Agg" column and "Total Amount" in the "Heading Text" column (Fig. 6.07).

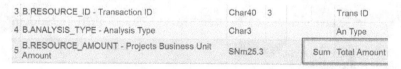

Fig 6.07

Before moving on to the next task, let us re-order field RESOURCE_ID so that it is #4 in the order. (Hint: Follow Step 03 from Chapter 5 - Fig. 5.13 to Fig 5.15).

Now let us apply the "aggregate" to RESOURCE_ID in order to obtain the row-count:

- Click on the "Edit" button as in Fig 6.05 – this time against field B.RESOURCE_ID.

- You will be taken to the "Edit Field Properties" page — Fig 6.08a.

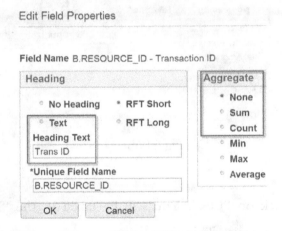

Fig 6.08a

- In the Heading group box, select "Text" and enter a value in the "Heading Text" field (Fig 6.08b). In our example, we will enter "Row Count" in that field in place of "Trans ID".

58

Edit Field Properties

Field Name B.RESOURCE_ID - Transaction ID

Heading		Aggregate
○ No Heading ○ RFT Short		○ None
[*] Text ○ RFT Long		○ Sum
Heading Text		* Count
Row Count		○ Min
*Unique Field Name		○ Max
B.RESOURCE_ID		○ Average

OK   Cancel

Fig 6.08b

- In the Aggregate group box, select "Count".

- Click on "OK". You will be taken to the "Fields" page again. This time, in our example, you will see "Sum" in the "Agg" column and "Total Amount" in the "Heading Text" column (Fig. 6.09).

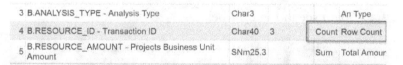

3	B.ANALYSIS_TYPE - Analysis Type	Char3		An Type
4	B.RESOURCE_ID - Transaction ID	Char40	3	Count Row Count
5	B.RESOURCE_AMOUNT – Projects Business Unit Amount	SNm25.3		Sum Total Amour

Fig 6.09

Step 03.   Criteria - Prompts

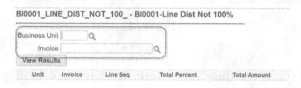

Fig 6.10

"Prompts" are entry points provided when the query is run (Fig 6.10). These are called runtime parameters. For example, in the case of the record PROJECT, if I need data for any value of PROJECT_ID, I can write a query that extracts data for all projects and look for the one that I need, or I can create a prompt to allow me to specify the value of PROJECT_ID each time I run the query.

Prompts can also be used to pass values programmatically to a query using peoplecode, where the query is used to extract data into a reporting tool such as BI Publisher. We will not cover this feature in the current book.

We will create 2 criteria lines using prompts to extract parameters to filter against.

- Click on the "Criteria" tab. It should resemble what you see in Fig 6.11 below.

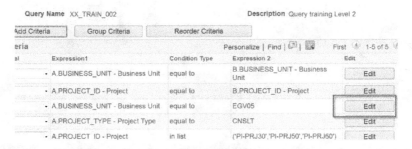

Fig 6.11

- Click on the "Edit" button as marked in Fig 6.11 - against A.BUSINESS_UNIT equal to EGV05

- The "Edit Criteria Properties" page appears (Fig 6.12).

- In the "Choose Expression 2 Type" change the selection from "Constant" to "Prompt" – a "Define Prompt" group box appears on the right.

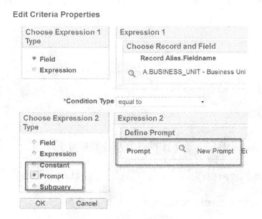

Fig 6.12

- Click on the "New Prompt" hyperlink.

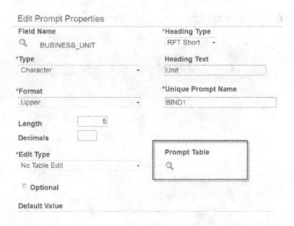

Fig 6.13

- Click on the Q icon below "Prompt Table" (Fig

6.13). The "Select a Prompt Table" page appears.

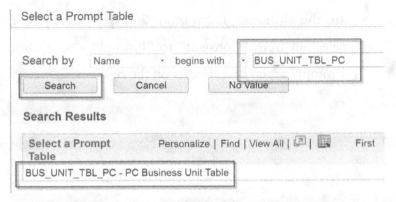

Fig 6.14

- Enter "BUS_UNIT_TBL_PC" (Fig 6.14) and click on the "Search" button. "BUS_UNIT_TBL_PC" appears in the search results.

- Select "BUS_UNIT_TBL_PC" in the Search Results. The "Edit Prompt properties" pop-up appears with the prompt table value populated (Fig 6.15).

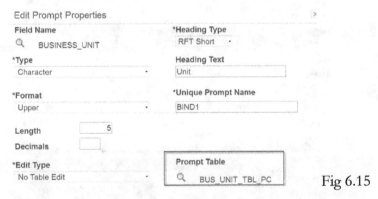

Fig 6.15

- Click on "OK". The "Edit Criteria Properties" page appears. The Prompt has ":1" (bind variable).

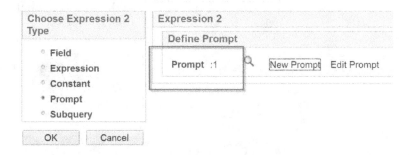

Fig 6.16

- Click on "OK" to get back to the "Criteria" page (Fig. 6.17). Note that the criteria for the BUSINESS_UNIT row has changed.

Add Criteria		Group Criteria	Reorder Criteria	

Criteria				Personalize | Find | 🖾
Logical		Expression1	Condition Type	Expression 2
	·	A.BUSINESS_UNIT - Business Unit	equal to ·	B.BUSINESS_UNIT - I Unit
AND	·	A.PROJECT_ID - Project	equal to	B.PROJECT_ID - Proj
AND	·	A.BUSINESS_UNIT - Business Unit	equal to	:1
AND	·	A.PROJECT_TYPE - Project Type	equal to	CNSLT

Fig 6.17

- Save your query.

Step 04.   Criteria - Subquery

A subquery is a query used within the criteria of an existing query in order to obtain values to filter the data against. In our current example, we will filter the data by projects that exist in the table "CA_DETAIL_PROJ".

- Click on the "Criteria" tab. It should resemble what you see in Fig 6.18 below.

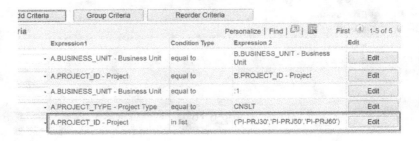

Fig 6.18

- Click on the "Edit" button as marked in Fig 6.18 - against A.PROJECT_ID.

Fig 6.19

- The "Edit Criteria Properties" page appears.

- In the "Choose Expression 2 Type" change the selection from "Constant" to "Subquery" – a "Define Subquery" group box appears on the right (Fig 6.19).

- Click on the "Define / Edit Subquery" hyperlink. The

"Records" Page appears.

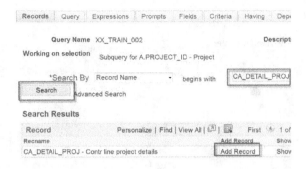

Fig 6.20

- Enter "CA_DETAIL_PROJ" and click on the "Search" button. The record - "CA_DETAIL_PROJ" will appear in the search results.

- Click on the "Add Record" hyperlink (Fig 6.20). The "Query" page appears (Fig 6.21).

Fig 6.21

- Click on the "Select" hyperlink (Fig 6.21) next to PROJECT_ID. The "Fields" page appears (Fig 6.22) with the PROJECT_ID field populated.

Fig 6.22

- Save your query.

- Click on the "Query" tab. The "Query" page appears as in Fig 6.23.

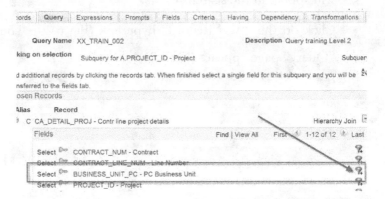

Fig 6.23

- Click on the 🎇 icon (Fig 6.23) on the far right - in line with field BUSINESS_UNIT_PC. The "Edit Criteria Properties" page appears.

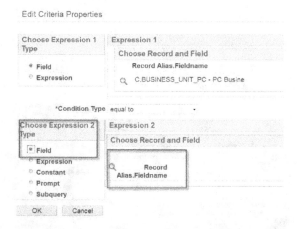

Fig 6.24

- In the Expression 2 group box, select "Field".

- Click on the 🔍 icon in the "Choose Record and Field" box. A pop-up page appears (Fig 6.25a).

Fig 6.25a

- Click on A.BUSINESS_UNIT to create criteria to compare A.BUSINESS_UNIT with the value from the subquery - C.BUSINESS_UNIT_PC.

Edit Criteria Properties

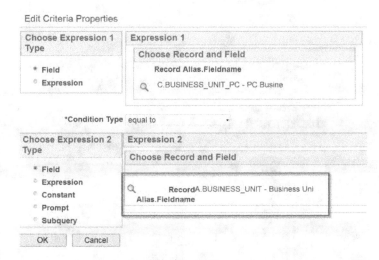

Fig 6.25b

- The "Edit Criteria Properties" page appears with the field A.BUSINESS_UNIT populated (Fig 6.25b)

- Click on "OK". The "Criteria" page appears with a row added (Fig 6.26).

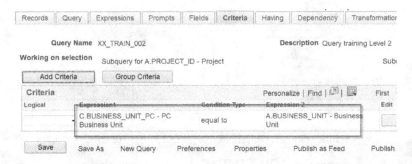

Fig 6.26

- Save your query.

Let's navigate back to the main Query.

68

- Click on the "Query" tab (Page 6.21).

- Click on the hyperlink "Subquery / Union Navigation". A pop-up appears as in Fig. 6.27.

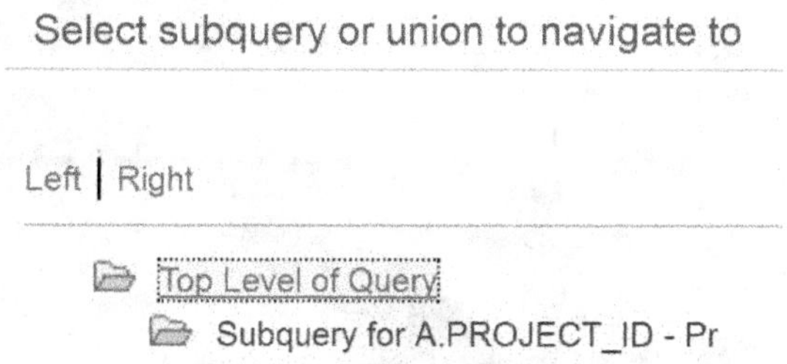

Select subquery or union to navigate to

Left | Right

📂 Top Level of Query
    📂 Subquery for A.PROJECT_ID - Pr

Fig 6.27

- Click on "Top Level of Query". The Main Query appears.

- Save your query.

We will delete a criteria line that we do not need for this exercise before we run our query.

- Click on the "Criteria" tab.

- Delete the criteria line of A.PROJECT_TYPE (Fig 6.28) by clicking on the ⊟ icon at the far right of the row.

Query Name XX_TRAIN_002   Description Query training Level 2

Working on selection   Top Level of Query   Subquery/Union Navigatic

| Add Criteria | Group Criteria | Reorder Criteria |

Criteria				Personalize | Find |	First 1-5 of 5 Last	
Logical	Expression1		Condition Type	Expression 2	Edit	Delete
	• A.BUSINESS_UNIT - Business Unit		equal to	B.BUSINESS_UNIT - Business Unit	Edit	–
AND	• A.PROJECT_ID - Project		equal to	B.PROJECT_ID - Project	Edit	–
AND	• A.BUSINESS_UNIT - Business Unit		equal to		Edit	–
AND	• A.PROJECT_TYPE - Project Type		equal to	CNSLT	Edit	–
AND	• A.PROJECT_ID - Project		in list	SUBQUERY	Edit	–

| Save | Save As | New Query | Preferences | Properties | Publish as Feed | Publish as Pivot Grid |

Fig 6.28

- Save your query.

Step 05.   Test your Skill

- Add one more criteria to this Query using the specifications listed below:

  i. Criteria Field – PROJECT_ID

  ii. Condition Type – In List

  iii. Criteria values - PI-PRJ30, PI-PRJ50, PI-PRJ60

- After completing the test above, continue to the next step to run the query and compare the result.

- Hint: The Solution is in Step 04 of Chapter 5.

Step 06.   Run Query XX_TRAIN_002

Now let us run this query and analyze the result.

- Click on the "Run" tab – a pop-up appears with a prompt for a Business Unit (Fig 6.29).

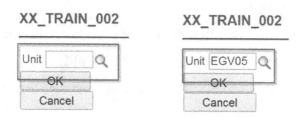

Fig 6.29

- Enter "EGV05" and click on "OK" - the "Run" page appears with your result (Fig 6.30).

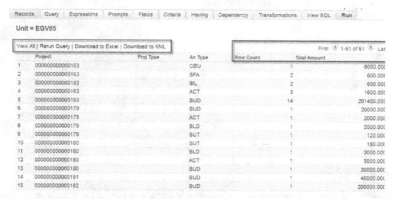

Fig 6.30

- You will notice that:

    i. The data is filtered to BUSINESS_UNIT = 'EGV05'

    ii. The result has rows even where PROJECT_TYPE is blank

    iii. We see a Total amount for every combination of PROJECT_ID, PROJECT_TYPE and ANALYSIS_TYPE that has met the specified criteria.

iv. We see a Row Count for every combination of PROJECT_ID, PROJECT_TYPE and ANALYSIS_TYPE that has met the specified criteria.

- Compare the result with Table 6.01.

Chapter 7: Level Three – Expressions

The "Expressions" feature of Query manager allows us to perform complex operations within a query by introducing SQL clauses in a text form. We will provide one such example in this chapter.

A. Objective

The objective of this chapter is to:

a) Show the working of the "Distinct" flag

b) Show the workings of Expressions by adding Fields:

- Summary Budget Amount

- Summary Expense Amount

- Variance (Budget – Actual)

c) Run these queries and analyze the results

B. Create Query – XX_TRAIN_003

Step 01.   Copy Query.

- Navigate to PeopleSoft Query Manager.

- Enter XX (Or your initials) in the search box.

- Click on the "Search" button. The Query "XX_TRAIN_002" will appear in the list.

- Click on "Edit"

- You will be transferred to the "Fields" page.

- Click on "Save As". A pop-up page appears.

- Populate the values as in Fig 7.01 and click on "OK".

Enter a name to save this query as:

*Query	XX_TRAIN_003
Description	Query training Level 3
Folder	
*Query Type	User
*Owner	Public

Query Definition:
- Training Exercise - Including Distinct Flag

| OK | Cancel |

Fig 7.01

- The Query is saved as XX_TRAIN_003

Step 02.   Delete Fields.

For the purpose of this chapter, we will not need the Aggregate fields set up in chapter 6. We will need to delete them.

- To proceed with this step, confirm that you are at the "Fields" page (Fig 7.02). If you are not at the "Fields" page, click on the "Fields" tab to get there.

Fig 7.02

- Delete rows 3, 4 and 5 by clicking on the ⊟ icon (Fig. 7.02).

- Click on the "Having" tab

- Delete the criteria row on this page by clicking on the ⊟ icon.

- Save your query.

Step 03.   Use of the "Distinct" flag.

The "Distinct" clause in a SQL statement reduces duplicate values in your extract. If your original extract had 10 rows with the same combination of fields, a distinct in your statement will reduce it to one row. To set up your query with the "distinct" feature, follow the steps below.

- Click on the "Properties" hyperlink at the bottom of the page. A pop-up appears.

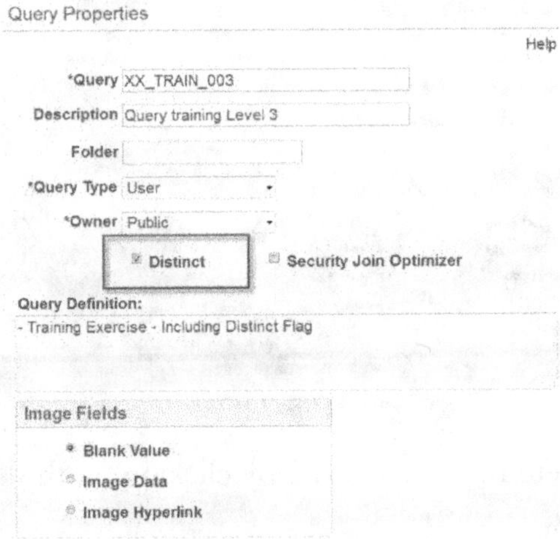

Query Properties

Help

*Query XX_TRAIN_003

Description Query training Level 3

Folder

*Query Type User

*Owner Public

☑ Distinct   ☐ Security Join Optimizer

Query Definition:
- Training Exercise - Including Distinct Flag

Image Fields
  ● Blank Value
  ○ Image Data
  ○ Image Hyperlink

Fig 7.03

- Click on the "distinct" checkbox (Fig 7.03).

- Click on OK

- Save your Query.

- Run your Query – a Prompt box appears.

- Enter 'EGV05' as the Business Unit and click on
  "OK". The result will be 14 rows of unique
  combinations as in Table 7.01.

Table 7.01	
PROJECT_ID	PROJECT_TYPE
000000000000163	
000000000000179	
000000000000180	
000000000000181	
000000000000182	
000000000000194	

000000000000195	
CWBPC1	
CWBPC100	
PI-PRJ30	
PI-PRJ50	CNSLT
PI-PRJ10	INTER
PI-PRJ60	R&D
PI-PRJ61	R&D

C. Create Query – XX_TRAIN_004

Step 01.   Copy Query.

- Navigate to PeopleSoft Query Manager.

- Enter XX (Or your initials) in the search box.

- Click on the "Search" button. The Query "XX_TRAIN_003" will appear in the list.

- Click on "Edit"

- You will be transferred to the "Fields" page.

- Click on "Save As". A pop-up appears.

- Populate the values as in Fig 7.01 and click on "OK".

Enter a name to save this query as:

*Query	XX_TRAIN_004
Description	Query training Level 4
Folder	
*Query Type	User
*Owner	Public

Query Definition:
- Training Exercise - Includes Expressions

OK	Cancel

Fig 7.04

- The Query is saved as XX_TRAIN_004

Step 02.   Uncheck the "Distinct" flag.

To study "Expressions", we will need the "Distinct" flag to be off by following the steps below.

- Click on the "Properties" hyperlink. A pop-up appears.

- Click on the "distinct" checkbox to uncheck it.

- Click on OK

- Save your Query.

Step 03.   Setup Budget Summary

Now that we have a Query with 2 fields PROJECT_ID and PROJECT_TYPE, we can set up the "Expression".

78

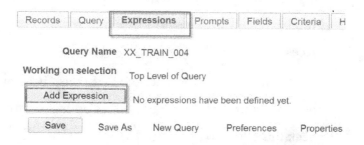

Fig 7.05

- Click on the "Expressions" Tab. The "Expressions" page will appear (Fig. 7.05).

- Click on the "Add Expression" button - the "Edit Expression Properties" page will appear (Fig. 7.06).

- Select Expression Type, Length & decimals. This will depend on the output that you expect for this field.

Edit Expression Properties

*Expression Type

| Signed Number | Length | 25 |
| Aggregate Function | Decimals | 2 |

Expression Text

```
CASE
WHEN B.ANALYSIS_TYPE = 'BUD' THEN
B.RESOURCE_AMOUNT
WHEN B.ANALYSIS_TYPE <> 'BUD' THEN 0
END
```

Add Prompt   Add Field

OK   Cancel

Fig 7.06

- In our example (Fig 7.06), our output is a "Signed Number" field with length of 22 and with 2 decimal places.

- Check the Aggregate checkbox if this field will contain summary data (Fig 7.06). For our example, check this checkbox.

- In the Expression Text box, enter the code that drives this expression. In our example, we have used the SQL - "CASE WHEN...END" clause to do a selective total of Budget amounts (Table 7.02).

Table 7.02
CASE WHEN B.ANALYSIS_TYPE = 'BUD' THEN B.RESOURCE_AMOUNT WHEN B.ANALYSIS_TYPE <> 'BUD' THEN 0 END

- Click on "OK". The "Expressions" page will appear again (Fig 7.07).
- Save your Query.

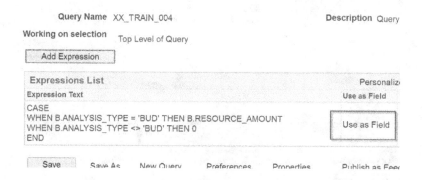

Fig 7.07

- If you intend to use this as one of the "Criteria", click on the filter icon (⁊) and proceed to create criteria in the same manner as you did in Chapter 6. In our example, we will <u>not</u> click on the filter icon.

- If you intend to use this as a field in your Query, click on the "Use as Field" hyperlink (Fig 7.07). In our example, we will click on the "Use as Field" hyperlink:

- Click on the "Fields" tab to get to the "Fields" page (Fig 7.08). Note that the Expression is now the last field in this list. The heading text is a short version of the Code in the expression.

- Click on the "Edit" button to make final changes to the expression as a field (Fig 7.08).

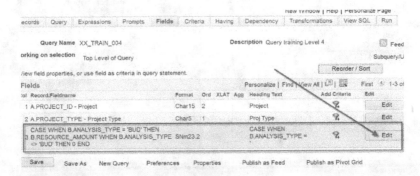

Fig 7.08

- The "Edit Field Properties" pop-up appears (Fig 7.09).

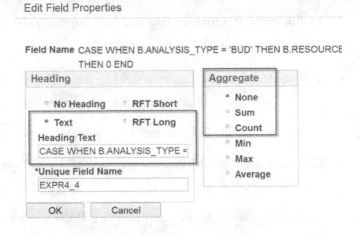

Fig 7.09

- Change the heading text — in our example, we will change the Heading Text field to "Budget" (Fig 7.10).

- Change the "Aggregate" option — in our example, we will change the "Aggregate" option to "Sum" (Fig

7.10).

Edit Field Properties

Field Name CASE WHEN B.ANALYSIS_TYPE = 'BUD' THEN B.RESOUR
THEN 0 END

Heading		Aggregate
○ No Heading ○ RFT Short		○ None
		✱ Sum
✱ Text ○ RFT Long		○ Count
Heading Text		○ Min
Budget		○ Max
*Unique Field Name		○ Average
EXPR4_4		

| OK | Cancel |

Fig 7.10

- Click on OK. You will be taken to the "Fields" page again. This time, in our example, you will see "Sum" in the "Agg" column and "Budget" in the "Heading Text" column for the updated Expression (Fig. 7.11).

Fields   Personalize | F

Col	Record.Fieldname	Format	Ord	XLAT	Agg	Heading Text
1	A.PROJECT_ID - Project	Char15	2			Project
2	A.PROJECT_TYPE - Project Type	Char5	1			Proj Type
3	CASE WHEN B.ANALYSIS_TYPE = 'BUD' THEN B.RESOURCE_AMOUNT WHEN B.ANALYSIS_TYPE <> 'BUD' THEN 0 END	SNm23.2			Sum	Budget

Fig 7.11

- Save your query.

- Click on the "Run" tab to run this query. The result

should contain data as in Table 7.03

Table 7.03		
PROJECT_ID	**PROJECT_TYPE**	**BUDGET**
000000000000163		201450.00
000000000000179		20000.00
000000000000180		30000.00
000000000000181		40000.00
000000000000182		200000.00
000000000000194		15000.00
000000000000195		300000.00
CWBPC1		100000.00
CWBPC100		1100000.00
PI-PRJ30		44312000.00
PI-PRJ50	CNSLT	5016000000.00
PI-PRJ10	INTER	40400.00
PI-PRJ60	R&D	1156000.00
PI-PRJ61	R&D	471000.00

Step 04.   Setup Expense Summary

Now we will set up a field for "Expense" summary – using "Expressions"

- Click on the "Expressions" Tab. The "Expressions" page will appear.

- Click on "Add Expression" - the "Edit Expression Properties" page will appear.

- Populate the page as in Fig 7.12.

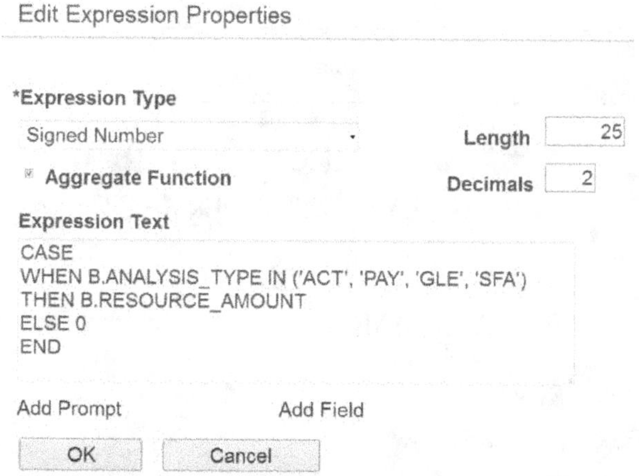

Edit Expression Properties

---

*Expression Type

| Signed Number | ▾ | **Length** | 25 |

☑ **Aggregate Function**   **Decimals** 2

Expression Text

```
CASE
WHEN B.ANALYSIS_TYPE IN ('ACT', 'PAY', 'GLE', 'SFA')
THEN B.RESOURCE_AMOUNT
ELSE 0
END
```

Add Prompt   Add Field

| OK | | Cancel |

Fig 7.12

- In our example (Fig 7.12), B.ANALYSIS_TYPE IN ('ACT', 'PAY', 'GLE', 'SFA') represents the Analysis Types on Expense-rows in PROJ_RESOURCE.

- Enter the

    i.   Expression Type,

    ii. Length and

    iii. Decimals

    as in Fig. 7.12.

- Check the Aggregate checkbox.

- In the Expression Text box, enter the code that drives this expression (Table 7.04).

- Click on "OK". The "Expressions" page will appear again.

Table 7.04
CASE
WHEN B.ANALYSIS_TYPE IN ('ACT',
'PAY', 'GLE', 'SFA') THEN
B.RESOURCE_AMOUNT
ELSE 0
END

- Save your Query.

- Click on the "Use as Field" hyperlink:

- Click on the "Fields" tab to get to the "Fields" page.

- Click on the "Edit" button to make final changes to the expression as a field. The "Edit Field Properties" pop-up appears.

- Change the heading text — in our example, we will change the Heading Text field to "Expense" (Fig 7.13).

- Change the "Aggregate" option — in our example, we will change the "Aggregate" option to "Sum" (Fig 7.13).

Edit Field Properties

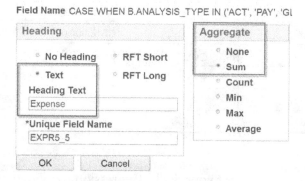

Fig 7.13

- Click on OK. You will be taken to the "Fields" page again. This time, in our example, you will see "Sum" in the "Agg" column and "Expense" in the "Heading Text" column for the updated Expression

- Save your query.

- Click on the "Run" tab to run this query. The result should contain data as in Table 7.05

Table 7.05			
PROJECT_ID	PROJECT_TYPE	BUDGET	Expense
000000000000163		201,450.00	2,200.00
000000000000179		20,000.00	2,000.00
000000000000180		30,000.00	3,000.00
000000000000181		40,000.00	-
000000000000182		200,000.00	4,004.00
000000000000194		15,000.00	-

000000000000195		300,000.00	-
CWBPC1		100,000.00	27,301.54
CWBPC100		1,100,000.00	1,065.12
PI-PRJ30		44,312,000.00	6,000,000.00
PI-PRJ50	CNSLT	5,016,000,000.00	801,000,000.00
PI-PRJ10	INTER	40,400.00	40,400.00
PI-PRJ60	R&D	1,156,000.00	528,000.00
PI-PRJ61	R&D	471,000.00	112,500.00

Step 05.   Test your Skill - Expression for Variance

Here is an exercise for you:

- Delete field PROJECT_TYPE

- Add a field "Variance" that displays the Budget available for each project (i.e. Budget – Expense).

- Hint: Use the Expression text as in Table 7.06.

Table 7.06
CASE
WHEN B.ANALYSIS_TYPE IN ('ACT',
'PAY', 'GLE', 'SFA') THEN
B.RESOURCE_AMOUNT * -1
WHEN B.ANALYSIS_TYPE = 'BUD'
THEN B.RESOURCE_AMOUNT
ELSE 0
END

- Save your query.

- Click on the "Run" tab to run this query. The result should contain data as in Table 7.05

Table 7.05			
PROJECT_ID	**BUDGET**	**EXPENSE**	**VARIANCE**
000000000000163	201,450.00	2,200.00	199,250.00
000000000000179	20,000.00	2,000.00	18,000.00
000000000000180	30,000.00	3,000.00	27,000.00
000000000000181	40,000.00	-	40,000.00
000000000000182	200,000.00	4,004.00	195,996.00
000000000000194	15,000.00	-	15,000.00
000000000000195	300,000.00	-	300,000.00
CWBPC1	100,000.00	27,301.54	72,698.46
CWBPC100	1,100,000.00	1,065.12	1,098,934.88
PI-PRJ30	44,312,000.00	6,000,000.00	38,312,000.00
PI-PRJ50	5,016,000,000.00	801,000,000.00	4,215,000,000.00
PI-PRJ10	40,400.00	40,400.00	-
PI-PRJ60	1,156,000.00	528,000.00	628,000.00
PI-PRJ61	471,000.00	112,500.00	358,500.00

CHAPTER 8: SQL REVIEW

In this chapter we will look at the SQL created by our queries.

A. View SQL page in PeopleSoft Query Manager

The "View SQL" page is used to review your SQL for correctness (if you are familiar with the structure of SQL). This page will also enable you to copy the SQL and run it in SQL Developer, Toad, Golden, or any other SQL tool at times when the volume of data extracted is high.

Step 01.   Navigation

- Navigate to Query Manager using the directions in Chapter 5.

- Click on the View SQL page.

- Compare the SQL in your query with the respective SQLs provided below.

Step 02.   XX_TRAIN_001

Table 8.01
SELECT A.PROJECT_ID, A.PROJECT_TYPE, B.RESOURCE_ID, B.ANALYSIS_TYPE, B.RESOURCE_AMOUNT FROM PS_PROJECT A, PS_PROJ_RESOURCE B WHERE (A.BUSINESS_UNIT = B.BUSINESS_UNIT AND A.PROJECT_ID = B.PROJECT_ID AND A.BUSINESS_UNIT = 'EGV05' AND A.PROJECT_TYPE = 'CNSLT' AND A.PROJECT_ID IN ('PI-PRJ30','PI-PRJ50','PI- PRJ60')) ORDER BY 2, 1, 3

Step 03.   XX_TRAIN_002

Table 8.02
SELECT A.PROJECT_ID, A.PROJECT_TYPE, B.ANALYSIS_TYPE, COUNT(*), SUM(B.RESOURCE_AMOUNT) FROM PS_PROJECT A, PS_PROJ_RESOURCE B WHERE (A.BUSINESS_UNIT = B.BUSINESS_UNIT AND A.PROJECT_ID = B.PROJECT_ID AND A.BUSINESS_UNIT = :1 AND A.PROJECT_ID IN (SELECT C.PROJECT_ID FROM PS_CA_DETAIL_PROJ C WHERE C.BUSINESS_UNIT_PC = A.BUSINESS_UNIT)) GROUP BY A.PROJECT_ID, A.PROJECT_TYPE, B.ANALYSIS_TYPE HAVING (COUNT(*) > '1') ORDER BY 2, 1

Step 04.   XX_TRAIN_003

Table 8.03

```
SELECT DISTINCT A.PROJECT_ID, A.PROJECT_TYPE
FROM PS_PROJECT A, PS_PROJ_RESOURCE B
WHERE ( A.BUSINESS_UNIT = B.BUSINESS_UNIT
AND A.PROJECT_ID = B.PROJECT_ID
AND A.BUSINESS_UNIT = :1
AND A.PROJECT_ID IN (SELECT C.PROJECT_ID
FROM PS_CA_DETAIL_PROJ C
WHERE C.BUSINESS_UNIT_PC = A.BUSINESS_UNIT))
ORDER BY 2, 1
```

Step 05.   XX_TRAIN_004

Table 8.04

```
SELECT A.PROJECT_ID, A.PROJECT_TYPE, SUM( CASE
WHEN B.ANALYSIS_TYPE = 'BUD' THEN
B.RESOURCE_AMOUNT
WHEN B.ANALYSIS_TYPE <> 'BUD' THEN
0
END), SUM( CASE
WHEN B.ANALYSIS_TYPE IN ('ACT', 'PAY', 'GLE', 'SFA')
THEN B.RESOURCE_AMOUNT
ELSE 0
END), SUM( CASE
WHEN B.ANALYSIS_TYPE IN ('ACT', 'PAY', 'GLE', 'SFA')
THEN B.RESOURCE_AMOUNT * -1
WHEN B.ANALYSIS_TYPE = 'BUD' THEN
```

```
B.RESOURCE_AMOUNT

ELSE 0

END)

FROM PS_PROJECT A, PS_PROJ_RESOURCE B

WHERE ( A.BUSINESS_UNIT = B.BUSINESS_UNIT

AND A.PROJECT_ID = B.PROJECT_ID

AND A.BUSINESS_UNIT = :1

AND A.PROJECT_ID IN (SELECT C.PROJECT_ID

FROM PS_CA_DETAIL_PROJ C

WHERE C.BUSINESS_UNIT_PC = A.BUSINESS_UNIT))

GROUP BY A.PROJECT_ID, A.PROJECT_TYPE

ORDER BY 2, 1
```

CHAPTER 9: QUERY TRANSFORMATIONS

In this chapter we will look at Transformations - the ability to change the looks of your query without compromising on accuracy and without having to create a report definition. Use the basic example below only to understand the concept.

Step 01.   Copy your Query

- Navigate to Query Manager
- Locate and Open Query XX_TRAIN_004
- Save the Query as "XX_TRAIN_005"
- Change the criteria A.BUSINESS_UNIT=:1 to A.BUSINESS_UNIT=EGV05

Step 02.   Create a Transformation row

- Click on the "Transformations" tab.
- Click on the "Add XSLT" button.
- Enter Name: Test Template
- Enter Output Type: HTML
- Enter the contents of Table 9.02 in the XSLT box.
- Click on "OK". You will be taken back to the "Transformations" page and you will see a new row.
- Save your Query.

- Click on the "Preview" button – your report will appear in another browser.

Table 9.02

```
<?xml version="1.0" encoding="utf-8"?>
<xsl:stylesheet version="1.0"
xmlns:xsl="http://www.w3.org/1999/XSL/Transform">
<xsl:output method="html" encoding="utf-8" doctype-public="-
//W3C//DTD XHTML 1.0 Transitional//EN" doctype-
system="http://www.w3.org/TR/xhtml1/DTD/xhtml1-
transitional.dtd"/>
<xsl:template match="query/row">
<html xmlns="http://www.w3.org/1999/xhtml">
<head>
<meta http-equiv="Content-Type" content="text/html;
charset=utf-8"/>
<title>Untitled Document</title>
</head>
<body>
<h2>My Test Report</h2>
   <table border="1">
    <tr bgcolor="#9acd32">
     <th width="244" style="text-align:left" > Project </th>
     <th width="134" style="text-align:left">Type</th>
            <th width="156" style="text-align:left">Budget
Summary</th>
            <th width="151" style="text-align:left">Expense
Summary</th>
            <th width="148" style="text-align:left">Available
Budget</th> </tr>
<tr> <xsl:for-each select="PROJECT_ID"><xsl:value-of
select="PROJECT_ID"/></xsl:for-each>
<td><xsl:value-of select="PROJECT_ID"/></td>
    <td><xsl:value-of select="PROJECT_TYPE"/></td>
            <td><xsl:value-of select="EXPR4_4"/></td>
            <td><xsl:value-of select="EXPR5_5"/></td>
            <td><xsl:value-of select="EXPR6_6"/></td></tr>
   </table>
</body>
</html>
</xsl:template>
</xsl:stylesheet>
```

95

CHAPTER 10: GRANT SUITE TABLES

Below are some of the important tables used for reporting on grants:

Module	Field Name	Description / Purpose
AR	DEPOSIT_CONTROL	Deposit Control Information
AR	ITEM	Identifies the invoice/online pending item store original and balance of item.
AR	ITEM_ACTIVITY	Line information for Receivables Items
AR	ITEM_DST	Chartfield Distribution information for Receivables & Payments
AR	PAY_MISC_DST	Non Customer Payment Distribution
AR	PAYMENT	Customer Payment Information
AR	PAYMENT_ID_CUST	Payment Customer Identification
AR	PAYMENT_ID_ITEM	Payment Item Identification
AR	PENDING_ITEM	Billing Items in AR Prior to AR Update
BI	BI_ACCT_ENTRY	Billing subsystem accounting entries
BI	BI_HDR	Header information for Customer Bills
BI	BI_LINE	Line information for Customer Bills
BI	BI_LINE_DST	Billing Line Distribution information
BI	BI_LINE_TAX_DTL	Detail tax data for Bill lines
BI	CUST_ADDRESS	Customer Address Detail - CUST_ID, AGING_ID, AGING_CATEGORY, AGING_AMT
BI	CUST_AGING	Customer Aging Details
BI	CUST_CONTACT	Customer Contact Information - CUST_ID, ITEM, ITEM_DT, ITEM_AMT, PAYMENT_ID, PAYMENT_DT, PAYMENT_AMT
BI	CUST_DATA	Customer Info / Balances - Customer Details such as Customer Balance, Last Payment, Last Aged
BI	CUSTOMER	Stores the profile data for customers / sponsors.

Module	Field Name	Description / Purpose
BI	INTFC_BI	Load from Contracts Billing and Errors from the billing interface processing.
CA	CA_ACCTG_LN_PC	Entries generated in Project Costing based on Accounting Rules
CA	CA_BILL_PLAN	Bill Plan Table holding contract-billing defaults
CA	CA_BP_EVENTS	Schedule for fixed price invoices.
CA	CA_CONTR_HDR	Contract Header Information
CA	CA_DETAIL	Contract Line Information
CA	CA_DETAIL_DST	Contract Distribution Detail - Used for Contract- driven fixed price accounting process.
CA	CA_DETAIL_PROJ	Links Contracts & Awards to Project ID
CA	CA_DETAIL_UAR	Unbilled Accounts Receivable chartfield distribution for a contract line
CA	CA_PREPAID_TBL	Contracts Prepaid Balance Table
CA	CA_RATE	Contract Rate Set or Plan for each contract line
GM	GM_AWARD	Award Profile
GM	GM_AWD_ATTR	Award Attributes
GM	GM_AWD_CERT	Stores the certification on the award.
GM	GM_AWD_COMMENT	Stores comment to the award.
GM	GM_AWD_FUND_PD	Total awarded amount with dates.
GM	GM_AWD_KEYWORD	Keywords associated to the award.
GM	GM_AWD_MILE	Links Milestone (Reporting requirements) on the award.
GM	GM_AWD_MOD	Stores all Award Modification for the award.
GM	GM_BUD_FA_HDR	F&A Rate Information for the proposal.
GM	GM_BUD_FA_RATE	Stores the Rate Type and Rate % on the proposal by project.
GM	GM_BUD_PERIOD	Proposal's F&A and total amount by periods.

Module	Field Name	Description / Purpose
GM	GM_FA_BASE_CAT	Stores the budget categories for the FA Base.
GM	GM_PRJ_ACT_FA	Post Award F&A Rate Type
GM	GM_PRJ_DEPT	Post Award Project Department
GM	GM_PRJ_ERR	F&A Errors for projects.
GM	GM_PROP_CERT	Stores the certification on the proposal.
GM	GM_PROP_KEY	Keywords associated to the proposal.
GM	GM_PROP_PROF	List name of those on the proposal and their role on the proposal.
GM	GM_PROP_PROJ	Temp project and or created project to the proposal.
GM	GM_PROPOSAL	Grant Proposal Information
HR	JOB	EE Job History - HR Manager Information
HR	PERS_DATA_EFFDT	Effective Dated Personal Data
KK	KK_ACTIVITY_LOG	This table gets populated when source transactions are budget checked
KK	KK_BUDGET_HDR	Budget Transfer and Budget Entry Journal Header details
KK	KK_BUDGET_LN	Budget Transfer and Budget Entry Journal line details
KK	KK_SOURCE_HDR	Associates the KK Transaction ID's with module specific Ids, like Journal ID & Voucher ID
KK	KK_SOURCE_LN	Contains actuals, encumbrances and pre-encumbrances transaction details.
KK	LEDGER_KK	Commitment Control summarized transaction balances.
PC	PC_BUD_DETAIL	Post Award Project Budget Detail
PC	PROJ_ACTIVITY	Project Activities
PC	PROJ_RESOURCE	Stores all transaction for grants, use to calculate the F&A and billing.
PC	PROJECT	Project Profile
PC	PROJECT_DESCR	Project Description
PY	HR_ACCTG_LINE	Payroll Accounting Line